# *Behind The Wheel*

# *Peggy Thompson*

# Table of Contents

ISBN: 9798535139074
First Edition

*Dedicated to my 45-year-old son*
*Bennett H. Thompson*
*who loved the driving school as much as I did,*
*but died too early to get to live out his life.*

## Acknowledgments

I am grateful to many people who helped make this book a reality. After spending many years living in a drivers' education car, I had many stories that I wanted to write, but did not know how to begin. I had jotted down stories over the years and finally after retirement and the COVID-19 pandemic, I found the time. I actually had a friend from seventh grade who was living in New York and was an editor. Ed Cone offered to help me edit my stories and it was so great to connect with him again.

My good friends and neighbors, Deborah Walz and Dan Holland read them and helped to make some corrections. My youngest daughter, Britney Bouldin, took time from her three young children to help me organize the history. My friend Lou Ellen Treadway helped make my stories more colorful. My new friend, Richard McKeown who knew more about publishing than I did. My husband, Bill, who put up with me talking about my book all the time. He deserves special mention. Last but not least, Katheryn, my granddaughter who read my stories from the very beginning.

A big thank you goes out to all of them for I could not have done this book without the encouragement they all gave me.

# Introduction

For more than 40 years, I owned and operated a driving school in Little Rock, Arkansas. A driving instructor is not a common occupation and I am often asked how I ended up in that line of work.

My answer is never simple and usually takes some explaining. It's not every day a mother of four young children decides to become a driving instructor and ends up building a thriving business. But that's exactly what I did.

Teaching people to drive was more than a job to me. Much more. I have always enjoyed meeting and getting to know people, including those who are different from me and come from different backgrounds. In that respect, teaching people to drive was a grand adventure and a thoroughly enriching career. Not only was I able to meet so many people, but helping them develop a life skill – a potentially life-saving skill – was very gratifying. Any time you can combine a career with a love for people, you can hardly call it work! For me, it wasn't 40 years of working, but a lifetime of making friends and memories from the 22,300 students I taught to drive.

After doing something you love for so long, it's difficult to contemplate walking away. The decision to retire is a difficult one for many, including me. Teaching people to drive was a huge part of my identity.

Without it, I wondered who I would be and what I would do with my time. Honestly, I couldn't fathom my life without it.

Then everything changed. Life is funny that way. One day you can be going in one direction and then, suddenly, something happens and you find yourself going in the complete opposite direction. Sometimes things happen in life that make decisions for you or at least make the decision easier. This is exactly what happened with me and my decision to retire.

Two events happened in my life that took me to a place where I had to let some things go. I needed to take care of myself. First was the death of my oldest child. Bennett was 45 and was working with me at the driving school. He was helping a lot and I was enjoying all the fresh ideas he was bringing to the business. Then, he unexpectedly died right before Thanksgiving. This delivered a devastating blow that no parent wants to experience. Burying a child is never the proper order of things no matter how grown they are. Experiencing such grief is something only those who go through it can understand.

Shortly after, my father, who was 103, also died. Though my father's death was more expected and a more natural order of things, the combination of the two deaths was too much for me to handle. So, I decided that it was time for me to retire. Thankfully, my other son, Brock, and his wife, Niki, decided that they were ready to take over the business. Even though it was hard to walk away, it was comforting to know the business was staying in the family. This transfer made Thompson Driving School a third-generation family business.

After retiring, I began to reflect on my years in the car and all the wonderful people I had the opportunity to teach. I thought about the many wonderful experiences with all of those people. I made many lasting friendships and accumulated many interesting stories which I have treasured over the years. Throughout the years, I have told all of these colorful "Driver's Ed" stories and was frequently told that I needed to write a book. I typically agreed knowing that I had 40 years of material from which to draw from. In the back of my mind, I have always wanted to write these stories, but I never seemed to find the time to sit down and write them out formally.

Then the COVID-19 virus pandemic hit in 2020. I found myself with what seemed like an ocean of time. One would think that having what felt like unlimited time would be a good thing. But when it is forced upon you along with the specter of death to a pandemic virus, it is harder to see the good in it. To be honest, it was a very difficult time for me as well as others. I am a person who likes to go and do. I like, and need, to see and interact with people. COVID-19 forced me into a situation where my life came to a screeching halt. Many things I enjoyed about life were taken from me. Yes, I now had plenty of time, but there were moments when this ocean of time also felt like a sea of loneliness and sadness that threatened to drown me.

One day, I was on Facebook and I stumbled across a page called "View From My Window." On this page, anyone could post a picture from their window and tell where they were from and what they were experiencing during the pandemic. The pictures were beautiful and people posted from all over the world. This quickly became my escape from the sadness and fear of the pandemic.

When I would look at these posts from strangers, it was if I left my house and was traveling all over the world. Looking out all their windows, it reminded me of my years of looking out the window of my car and seeing all the sights of my city. I decided to use this time of quarantine and isolation to compile stories to share the view from my car window with the world. My hope is that these stories will touch your life just as the people in them touched mine.

*Peggy Thompson*
*Little Rock, Arkansas*

# Part One:
## Getting Started

In 1976, my life changed. While I enjoyed life as a stay-at-home mother of four, I was interested in changing my routine. Anyone who has been a mother can tell you that it is simultaneously the hardest and most rewarding job there is. As with anything that is as challenging as motherhood, it is always good to get out and change the scenery. That is how teaching driving started for me. I thought it would be fun to get out of the house a little. I am very much a people person and I enjoy spending time with others. So, this was a way for me to get a change of scenery, recharge my battery and make a little extra money.

Fortunately, my husband's parents had started a driving school back in 1955. This allowed me to become part of it. It is important to note that we didn't join my in-law's school. Instead, we started a second school. I don't remember why we did it that way. Looking back on it now, it seems strange, and strangely enough, there was even a period when I was answering the phones for both schools.

To get started, we had to take a few driver's education classes at the University of Central Arkansas in Conway, about an hour's drive from my home in Little Rock. Given we were starting a second school that was separate from my in-laws, we had to get our school accredited with the state of Arkansas. To do this, we had to go through the Arkansas State Board of Private Career Education to get our school accredited and ultimately receive our license to operate our driving school here in Arkansas.

With our new license in hand, we bought a car and equipped it with a brake on the passenger side of the front seat. We purchased magnetic signs to stick on the sides and back of the car. These signs were great for letting others know that there was a beginner driving the car and they also helped advertise our school. Another way that we advertised was by listing my business in the telephone book.

We named our school Little Rock Driving School. Later, after my in-laws retired, we took over the A-1 Thompson Driving School name. That meant we would be the first listing in the yellow pages and hopefully the school that people would call first. One of the things we advertised, and were proud of, was that we could teach anyone to drive. Our students included young drivers, elderly drivers, people from other countries, the hearing impaired and physically disabled, as well as children with special needs. We designed and customized our lessons to meet the needs of each student.

In the 1970s in Little Rock, driver education was taught in the public school system. Students took the class as an elective. Due to the large number of teenagers taking advantage of the schools' classes, our school was initially very small. After a few years, the local school district decided to discontinue driver education from its curriculum and our little school started to grow and

grow very quickly! In fact, we had to hire another instructor because there was no way we could personally teach all the students. Bear in mind, I was also managing all the work that comes with being a wife and mother of four. It was quite a juggling act and there were many times when the demands of motherhood were in direct conflict with the demands of the driving business. Often I felt like I needed to be in two places at one time, but I always managed to find a way.

One example of these times where I felt like I was being pulled in two different directions was when my third child, Beth, was diagnosed with asthma at seven-years-old. Her first asthma attack was very traumatic because we didn't know what was wrong and she felt like she was going to suffocate. After that, she was scared that it would happen again and was petrified for me to ever leave her. I had to get creative with my scheduling but finally worked something out. I would schedule some of the lessons early in the morning and would bring Beth with me. She was still sleepy enough that she would just lie down and sleep in the backseat of the car. Believe it or not, she would sleep very soundly back there. That is, until the student would hit the brake too hard and down Beth would roll onto the floor. There is no way that would be allowed today, and rightly so!

As Beth got older, she became less afraid and stopped going with me on the driving lessons. That was about the time when her younger sister, Britney, went through a similar phase and took naps in the back seat while I taught. She, too, would wake up by rolling onto the floor when a student hit the brake too hard. They are both mothers now and have children of their own. They both still talk about their time sleeping in the back seat of the driving car.

My husband and I taught together for about 12 years before divorcing. At that time, he branched out and established another school, which enabled me to take over the A-1 Thompson Driving School.

Throughout the years, we picked up students all over Little Rock, North Little Rock and sometimes as far as Conway and Hot Springs. In the beginning, there were no freeways in Little Rock. That meant, depending on where the student lived, it could take a while to pick up students for their lessons.

Thankfully, in those early days without freeways, there was not a lot of traffic. Most lessons lasted two hours from time of pick-up to time of drop off. Given that we picked up all over town, sometimes we would have a long way to travel to get to a place that was suitable for a beginner to safely learn to operate the car. We handled that by using the time it took to get to a safe location as a time to teach about the rules and regulations of the road and important facts about the car itself. Whether the student was sitting behind the wheel or not, all the time in the car was used as teaching time.

# Part Two:

## Changes Through
## The Years

## Part Two: Changes Through the Years

There are a lot of differences today compared with when I started. Initially our school was operated out of our home, making us ahead of our time in that respect! I was both the instructor, who was in the car all the time, and the office worker, who returned calls and scheduled the lessons. This meant that I needed to be in two places at one time. To solve that, I purchased an answering machine to record all the calls for the business while I was teaching in the car.

Once I returned home and after the kids went to bed, I would spend hours returning all the calls from that day. After 20 years, the school finally grew to a size where I needed to hire an employee to help run the office. I didn't feel like they would want to be in my house so I decided to rent an office. It really did make it feel more official.

Other things that changed were communication, advertising and forms of payment. In the 1970s, there were no cell phones. When I needed to make a call, I had to stop and use a pay phone. Additionally, there was no way for my kids to get in touch with me while I was in the car. I would periodically check on them from a pay phone to make sure everything was okay at home. As a mom who worries, I made it a point to know where all the pay phones were all over the city and I always had change in my car ready to go when needed. Needless to say, it was life-changing when cell phones came along.

Early on, we would collect payment through cash or check before we were able to accept credit and debit cards. Now, of course, those are the primary means of payment.

Also, since telephone books are no longer used, we have found alternative and innovative ways to advertise. Our best method of advertising has always been and continues to be word of mouth. A good reputation as a business is always your best advertisement. We also supplement our advertisement with fliers, school partnerships and social media.

Another thing that changed over the course of my 40 years teaching were the cars and what we taught because of those changes. When I started, there were no seatbelts. Once seatbelts became standard in cars, we started teaching and encouraging buckling up as the best choice for safety since wearing them wasn't required by law yet.

Many will recall that as late as the 1970s, there were no car seats for children. If the car had to stop suddenly, parents would stretch their arm out in front of the kids in an attempt to keep them from flying through the windshield. To this day, I still do that when suddenly stopping. Old habits do indeed die hard!

*Since Thompson Driving School was established, the metropolitan Little Rock, Arkansas area has grown from 169,000 in 1955 to 521,000 in 2021.*

Source: Macrotrends

Another difference about cars was that locking doors and rolling windows up and down were all done manually. Today's drivers have it so easy!

One of the biggest safety improvements to cars had a significant effect on the way we taught hand placement on the steering wheel. Initially, we taught our students to hold the wheel at 'ten and two.' This placement allowed for optimal control and maneuvering of the vehicle. However, that changed when cars became equipped with airbags. You see, if an airbag deploys while your hands are at ten and two, your hands could fly up and hit your face. To prevent that from happening, we began teaching hand placement on the wheel at 'three and nine.' This way, if the airbag deploys, it will push the driver's hands out to the side instead of toward their face. That is a word of advice to you older drivers!

The area where we did the bulk of our beginning lessons has also changed through the years. At the time we started teaching, Riverdale Country Club was moving from near downtown and the Arkansas River, to the western part of Little Rock and became the Pleasant Valley Country Club. When that happened, the old club grounds became an ideal area to teach driving because there wasn't much traffic. That is where we started teaching basic driving skills that we cover in the first lesson.

Now all these years later, this area has become built up with apartments and businesses, creating a lot of traffic. Additionally, the city's parks have improved and attract walkers, joggers and bikers enjoying the outdoor space. The increase in both car and pedestrian traffic has made it almost too busy to safely teach driving there.

Lastly, the faces working the business have also changed through the years. As my children grew up, at one time or another, they all learned to teach and help out with the school. All the kids learned at a very young age how to professionally give information over the phone and how to deliver very good customer service.

My daughter Beth managed the office for me while she was a new mom. That was when the office was still in my home and it was wonderful because she could bring her babies to work with her.

All four of my children have taught driving lessons at different times of their lives. I also had many non-family employees help me teach in the car and in the classroom over the years. Many of these instructors stayed with us so long that they ended up being like family.

While there have been many changes over the years, one thing that hasn't changed through the years is that Thompson Driving School was and continues to be a family business. I find that very gratifying.

# Part Three:
## My Stories

As I mentioned in the Introduction, among the greatest treasures and memories I have of my life and career are the people I've met and the experiences we have shared.

Throughout most of the remainder of my book, I want to share stories about some of the people, places and experiences I came to know from *Behind the Wheel.*

Early on in my career, I had a student who lived on Stagecoach Road in the southwestern part of Little Rock. On this occasion I picked up the student at their home and instead of heading to our usual behind-the-wheel training location at Murray Lock and Dam on the Arkansas River, we headed west on Stagecoach away from Little Rock.

Normally our lessons would take two hours. But since Stagecoach Road took us into some more rural, and quite attractive areas, I lost track of time! As a result, what was normally a two-hour lesson became a four-hour lesson. We wandered so far out Stagecoach Road that it took a while to get back to Little Rock. While I enjoyed the drive and ride, I learned a good lesson: Time flies when you're having fun ... and when you don't pay attention to the clock!

While the area known as Murray Lock and Dam was a great place for learning to drive, we always tried to keep in mind it is, after all, adjacent to the Arkansas River. This fact was made even clearer to me during one lesson. We were working on backing up and the student put the car in reverse. She then hit the gas instead of the brake, and we went flying toward the river, where we almost ended up.

Obviously, she thought she was on the brake when -- Surprise! -- she was on the gas. Believe it or not, it is not unusual for a new driver to confuse the brake and the gas. That is a lesson I always kept in mind and made sure not to assume there would be no such confusion. I made it a point after this particular incident to go over – once, twice, three times! – the difference between the brake pedal and the gas pedal.

Fortunately, I was able to hit the brake on the passenger side. But my student was pushing so hard on the gas that I was barely able to stop us. The expression "put your best foot forward" gained a new meaning for me. And when you are a driving instructor, your best foot is often the one that hits the brakes!

*The parking lot of the Murray Lock and Dam on the Arkansas River was an excellent place for students to begin their behind-the-wheel instruction. It was secluded and usually empty of cars.*

One day, I was with a student on Rodney Parham Road, one of Little Rock's busiest streets. We came upon a maroon Cadillac with a senior citizen behind the wheel.

I decided to use this opportunity to teach my student about senior citizen drivers. It is not unusual for them to drive large cars and drive slowly. It can be maddening to get stuck behind one!

As I was sharing this important information with my student driver, we pulled closer to the maroon Cadillac. It was then that I saw, to my shock, that my Dad was the driver. I was surprised to see him in Little Rock since my parents lived in a retirement community called Hot Springs Village, an hour away.

Hot Springs Village is a very safe place to drive because there is very little traffic, especially when compared to the state's largest city! Add to that the fact my Dad was ninety-nine years old at the time, and you can imagine my shock. Having said that, Dad was a very good driver, but I was still surprised, and amused, to learn he was the senior citizen who became an object lesson for my young driving student.

*My Dad, Jim McKinnon*

Sometime later, a reporter from the Hot Springs Village newspaper contacted me for help in writing an article about my Dad. I related the incident to the reporter about seeing him while he was driving in Little Rock. I told the reporter what I had taught my student about older drivers. I was concerned Dad would be upset with me when the article appeared with him as the unsuspecting subject.

I had put him in the class of older drivers, of which he did not consider himself a member. After all, he was only ninety-nine at the time! But he took it in stride and with good humor.

Dad finally gave up his car keys when he turned 100, which he said was the hardest thing he ever had to do. But it was a relief to me as it would be to any child of a 100-year-old parent that still drives.

However, Dad's driving career was not over. He got himself a golf cart so he could still drive around Hot Springs Village. My Dad was a gentleman in every sense of the word. He passed away at age 103 and always believed in staying active and on the move, even if it that meant taking a drive to the Big City every now and then.

One of my favorite students was a woman named Ann. She was quite the character. Ann would wait for me in an alley behind the apartment complex where she lived. She wore tattered clothes for every lesson and always sported some strange-looking boots. It appeared that she had just gotten out of bed!

Prior to coming to Arkansas and the United States, Ann had lived in Australia and Africa. She was a reader of, and believer in, the tabloid newspaper, National Enquirer.

After spending several hours teaching Ann, I learned that she had an interesting personal story that ended up bringing her to Little Rock. While living in Africa she became very sick and doctors there were unable to diagnose her condition satisfactorily.

Ann told me that she used a dating app and met a doctor that lived here in Little Rock. He became very interested in her case and made arrangements to bring her to America. After ordering a battery of tests for Ann, the doctor discovered she had a tapeworm in her stomach, which had been her problem all along.

Ann improved greatly after he treated her and eventually she married this doctor. Somehow, she managed to get her story into the National Enquirer. She moved to Hot Springs Village with her new husband and every Christmas since then, I have received a call from her.

One never knows where life, and love, will lead them!

Another of my favorite students was a petite lady named Virginia who I guessed to be about seventy years old. She was just five feet tall with short gray hair. Virginia was what we have come to recognize as a hoarder. Whenever I went into her apartment, I could not walk through the clutter.

She piled stacks of cereal boxes everywhere and there was no place to sit. Since Virginia had never driven, she took over sixty lessons from Thompson Driving School. Each lesson lasted two hours. That adds up to more than 120 hours, or five full days of driving lessons. Virginia was fun to teach because she was so enthusiastic about learning to drive.

When we both agreed she was a good enough driver, she bought a car. I thought I'd heard the last of Virginia after that, but one day I got a call from her. She wanted me to drive with her to Pine Bluff in her new car to visit relatives. Pine Bluff is about one hour south of Little Rock. I gave the matter a lot of thought before giving her my answer. I kept reminding myself that I would be a passenger in her car. That meant the passenger seat would have no brake, unlike my teaching cars. Yikes, I thought!

With misgivings I finally decided to accompany her. When I arrived at Virginia's apartment, she was out of breath and exhausted. Her fingernails were broken, and she was very upset. I asked her what had happened that she was in such a state.

Virginia explained she had reviewed her manual the night before to get her car ready for a road trip. For some reason, she decided she needed to remove all of the gravel from the treads of her tires.

I had no idea then, and still don't know how she misinterpreted the manual to do such a thing. I waited for her to catch her breath before we set out and she seemed to be in reasonable shape for the trip.

We drove to Pine Bluff and to this day I don't remember much about the trip. I don't even remember meeting her relatives. I was extremely nervous, to say the least.

Virginia was very proud to make it back home, and I was relieved the trip was over. That was the last time I saw Virginia. Sometime later I ran into a mutual acquaintance who asked if I remembered Virginia, as if I could forget her! My friend related that Virginia never got a ticket and never had a wreck. She enjoyed many years on the road thanks to my patience in sticking with her. Like my Dad, Virginia taught me it is never too late to learn something new if you have the will.

Even though I spent my career as an instructor of students, I learned something from most every one of them, too. There was one in particular who taught me as much about determination as I taught her about driving.

She was a fifteen-year-old girl born without arms. Her Dad had given her a little driving instruction before he sent her to us, so she had some experience. She was a very interesting child, who could do most anything. She began with one foot working the gas and the brake, and the other foot operating the steering wheel. It was quite a challenge for her as a driver and me as an instructor. It was amazing to watch her operate the gas, brake and steering wheel with just her feet. She was barefooted to allow a good grip on the wheel. She successfully learned all of the driving skills that we teach. These include speed recognition, traffic lights, traffic patterns, lane usage, one-way streets, and just being able to operate the car safely.

Thompson Driving School also offers a classroom lecture. The lecture helps students pass the written part of the driving test at the Arkansas State Police Headquarters. The lecture often leads to a discount on the parents' auto insurance. This student had already passed her driving test, but was taking the lecture for the discount on her insurance.

When she arrived at class in her car, the other students could hardly believe their eyes. She got out of the car carrying a little shoulder bag on the stump of her arm. As we began the lecture, she placed her foot on the table with a pencil between two toes and away she went taking notes.

Her classmates were very kind to offer her help, but she didn't need it. She was good at everything she attempted. We learned that she was an expert swimmer and diver as well. Special needs children are called "special," and for good reason. They seem to excel at anything they undertake. This inspiring girl overcame the odds and exceeded all our expectations.

What did she teach me and the other students? For one, attitude is as important as aptitude and for another, commitment beats complaining every time.

This fifteen-year-old will always have a special place in my heart, because she proves that just about anyone can learn to drive. I have never forgotten her and I doubt the students in that class have either.

I once taught another student with physical challenges. In her thirties, she was paralyzed on her right side and had to learn to use her left foot both for the gas and for the brake. Her husband was paralyzed and wheelchair-bound so she had to learn to drive. I will never forget this one either.

Most kids who learn to drive have the benefit of being able to practice driving with their parents. This student had no one to practice with except me. She ended up taking a lot of lessons. Though she was becoming a very good driver, she was still afraid to drive alone.

During our last lesson, I told her I needed some exercise and that I was going to get out of the car and let her drive up and down River Road while I walked. Of course, I would not have done this if I didn't know she was capable. Well, that's all it took. She became very confident and knew she was on her way. She was one of those students I would love to have followed up with to know what happened to her, but I never heard from her again.

**I** am not the only one with interesting stories about some of our students. One day, one of our new instructors had an interesting lesson with a student.

This student did not have a car and all she wanted to do was drive around the city with no particular destination in mind. And that is exactly what she and our instructor did. When the instructor returned the student to her apartment, a policeman was waiting for her at her front door. As you might imagine, she became very nervous. Especially when the policeman came to our instructor's car, opened it, and ordered the student out. It seems she was wanted for writing bad checks! In fact, the check that she had just written to pay for her driving lesson bounced. After this experience, my new instructor was not sure she wanted to continue teaching driving lessons.

I continued to receive calls from this troublesome student. She kept asking for another lesson, promising she would make good the bad check she had written earlier. We declined the offer, yet she continued to call. One time she identified herself as a doctor. Another time, she was a preacher.

This was in 2011 when she was sixty-five years old. This took place the last year before I retired. She became quite a problem, and we never did collect from her.

Fast forward ten years and I get a call from my son who took over the business when I retired. He wanted to know if I knew this lady by name. I knew exactly who he was talking about. I told him I thought she was trouble. She was ten years older by now and she was still trying to get free rides around town. My son decided not to do business with her even though she called the office and complained that he didn't want her business. It was interesting to me that after ten years, she played the same old game. It takes all kinds of people to make up the world, including frauds who bounce checks.

Thompson Driving School taught throughout the Little Rock metropolitan area which today has a population of 521,000. We also conducted training throughout the state of Arkansas, and the company continues to do so today.

While teaching a student on University Avenue, one of the city's major thoroughfares, I noticed an African-American man who stood tall and walked purposefully, yet slowly, while carrying a backpack. I continued to see him week after week in different areas of Little Rock.

One day when I was not teaching, I saw him and stopped to engage him in conversation. I wanted to hear his story and learn more about him. He was a war veteran and he explained that he walked every day to a different location for his mental and physical health. On Sundays, he played basketball with the kids downtown where he lived.

It was through this conversation we became "waving buddies." After I retired, I was driving and saw him, still walking. He had changed. He was gray and he looked much older, although he appeared to still be in good shape. He recognized me immediately and waved. A lifelong friend I had made from my car window and I never got his name.

I got a call from a father whose child was attending a local private school. He wanted to enroll his son in driving lessons but he requested that I not put "Student Driver" signs on the car. We use them for our own safety as well as for the safety of other drivers. The signs alert them there is a new driver behind the wheel. The Dad explained his son would be embarrassed if his friends, who were already driving, saw that he was driving with signs plastered on the car. In no uncertain terms, I informed him that we had to use the signs for everyone's safety.

This sign-averse young man was one of the most difficult students I ever had. When we called to set up his second lesson, his mother informed us that she did not feel he needed any more lessons. They had bought their prodigy his own car and she claimed that he was doing fine.

Somewhat to our surprise, she called back a few weeks later and admitted that her son needed lessons after all. He had totaled his car on the first day of school! We learned from this that parents sometimes need lessons in understanding, and guiding, their children, just as the kids need lessons in learning how to drive.

## PLEASE BE PATIENT
# STUDENT DRIVER

*Nearly every driver has seen a sign like this at some point while driving. Every now and then a teenage student would be embarrassed to be seen driving a car with this sign but after I explained that the signs were as much for their safety as for other drivers they came to appreciate the signs more.*

In addition to teaching our clients to drive, we sometimes had to deal with their issues. We designed special lessons for those students to help them overcome their problems.

One student in her late thirties would not drive anywhere that involved crossing a bridge. When she contacted us for help, we first had her practice driving to make sure she knew how to drive safely. Then we let her drive on the Broadway Bridge that crosses the Arkansas River and connects Little Rock and North Little Rock.

After driving across the bridge several times, she started gaining confidence. We then instructed her to drive across the Main Street Bridge. We spent about two hours per lesson doing nothing but driving back and forth across other bridges as well. It took several lessons, but she finally accomplished what we had set out to teach her: to not fear driving over a bridge. All she needed was for someone to drive with her to build up self-confidence. The lesson we learned is never give up on anyone who needs our help. This was a very interesting case. I am confident that she is still driving across bridges without fear.

*It is not uncommon for new drivers to have anxiety about driving across bridges, especially large ones like the Broadway Bridge, one of several bridges crossing the Arkansas River in Little Rock. My approach was to have students drive across the bridges until confidence replaced their fears.*

> Peggy,
>   Thank you for your time, patience and guidance.
>
>                 Joan Knox

> Mrs. Thompson,
>   Thank you for the wonderful professional service you provide. I knew Jared will be a better driver with the tools provided by your program.
>   The private lessons help me feel more assured that Jared will be a safe, responsible driver.   Sincerely, Lisa Brown

I received countless thank you notes over my 40 years as a driving instructor. The ones on this page and the next are just a few of them. I also received Christmas cards and Mothers Day cards from some of my students. I was always pleased to hear from them and learn that the experience of learning to drive was an important and memorable chapter in their lives.

1-13-99

Peggy –
Thank you again
for the great job that
you did with Amanda.
She really learned a
lot, and she enjoyed
her time with you.
We recommend
your services highly.

Sincerely,
Rhonda Potter

Behold, I make all things new.
Revelation 21:5 KJV

Peggy,
Thank you so
much. I tell
everyone to enroll
with you. Patrick
passed his test and
is doing well!
Thanks for doing
all 3 children.
Francie

115 WASHINGTON AVENUE · SANTA FE · NEW MEXICO 87501
TELEPHONE 505 988 3030 · FACSIMILE 505 983 3277

From the desk of Juanita Carter

Mrs. Thompson,
Thank you so
much for giving
Andrew a good start
to what we hope
will be good driving
practices.

Juanita Carter

Many children from out of town passed the summer in Little Rock with their grandparents. They might stay for a few weeks or the entire summer. The grandparents were always looking for ways to entertain them and children would sometimes ask to be allowed to drive. At home, their parents didn't take the time to teach them, and one thing about all grandparents, they want to make their grandchildren happy!

But after driving with them in parking lots a few times, the grandparents decided very quickly that they did not want the responsibility of teaching them. That's when we would get a call.

One of these kids was a talented, eighteen-year-old girl, who had just graduated from high school. She didn't know a thing about driving. As a singer, she had starred in many productions. She had one big fault: she was always late. I put up with this behavior for a while since she lived in Benton, a city thirty minutes from Little Rock. Since this would make me late for my next lesson, I finally made her understand that she could no longer be late.

She took many lessons throughout the summer and I came to know her well. She was a lot of fun to work with when she started being on time. Being on time was something she not only learned from me, but also from a cruise ship trip with her aunt. It seems she had gotten left behind on the shore as the ship sailed off. She had met someone on shore and partied all night, and then fell asleep on the beach. This cost her a couple of thousand dollars to catch up with the ship that had sailed off without her.

I can only imagine all the people on that ship watching as she caught up and got on board. To her credit, she got a job to repay the aunt for the expenses she incurred. She was quite an interesting student. She finally got her license after finishing her lessons and I never saw her again.

The lesson here whether you're driving or doing something: *Don't miss the boat!*

One summer, a granddaughter from Israel came to Little Rock to stay with her grandparents for the summer. The grandparents had moved to Little Rock from Israel years before. They owned a shop at Park Plaza, one of our biggest malls, called Joe's Hobby Shop. You could find just about anything at that store in the way of hobbies. I remember going there often as a child.

While I was teaching this beautiful young woman to drive, I asked her what she wanted to be when she grew up. I was astonished by her reply.

"I want to be the Prime Minister of Israel."

She was very smart and caught on to driving very quickly. I could actually see this young woman achieving anything she set out to do. I was also surprised to learn that since she had just graduated from high school, she would be going into the military. That is expected of girls in Israel after they finish school. She is one in particular I wish I had kept up with.

Some of the most challenging students at Thompson Driving School were from India. It was during my last ten years at the driving school that they started locating in the Little Rock area. A large pipeline company had brought them to Little Rock and offered them work.

Many had lots of self-confidence and they tried to convince us they knew how to drive. We learned that in India, driving meant going five miles an hour and honking. Apparently, it is not unusual in India for there to be only a few signs or directions on the roads. Thus, they really knew very little about driving.

Some of the Indians did not speak English. We needed an interpreter to communicate, and that was a very difficult way to teach. Interpreters sat in the back seat, leaning forward and repeating everything I said in their language.

In addition to pipeline workers, there were also doctors and computer programmers who usually spoke some English. There was also a community of Indians who owned motels and convenience stores.

I worked with one Indian for about twenty hours and he had a fascinating line of work. He was a magician! He and I drove to Benton for him to practice on the interstate after he learned the basics. We would stop for a soft drink and then drive back to Little Rock. He owned a motel downtown. He always invited me to come in and taste his wife's cookies. I went into the apartment and saw a white dove flying around. I assumed he used the dove for his magic. I went with him to the car dealership to buy a car. He had learned to drive in my Honda Civic, so that is what he wanted.

The Indian princesses, as we called the wives, always wanted to show me their wedding pictures. One Indian wife had just entered an arranged marriage. The "princesses" were among my most challenging students. They didn't understand that they did not have to turn the wheel so much. We would careen from one side of the road to the other. It was like a bad ride at an amusement park!

I was giving lessons at Murray Lock and Dam to an Indian student of ours. Murray Lock and Dam is where they lock the boats through on the Arkansas River. We would always start our lessons on this parking lot.

There were no cell phones at this time which meant I had to use pay phones to check in with my next student. On this particular day, I got out of the car and went to a nearby pay phone. As I was making the call, I noticed that my student was driving all over the parking lot. I was panicked because he was just a beginner. I hung up the phone and chased after him. That must have been a funny sight to behold! For some reason, I guess he felt authorized to practice while I was on the phone. I let him have it! I was sure he would never do it again. But I was wrong.

The same thing happened at the Arkansas State Police Headquarters a few days later when he went to take his driving test. The trooper had asked him to sit in his car and wait for the tester. Nevertheless, on his own he decided he could practice and started driving all around the parking lot. When the tester finally arrived for this student, he was nowhere to be found.

They finally found him driving all over the lot. This one got into a lot of trouble and, not surprisingly, failed the test.

I had a hair-raising experience with a fourteen-year-old boy who was only on his second lesson. Thus, he was a pretty new driver. We were driving toward downtown on Markham Street. This road is hilly and narrow with telephone poles on each side. There is no way to avoid the poles if you have to hit the shoulder for some reason.

As we came over one of the hills, a queen-size mattress appeared in the middle of the road. It must have fallen out of the back of a truck. I didn't have a moment to decide how to advise this young student. I just had to hope he would be resourceful enough to get through the situation without mishap. Fortunately, there was no one coming over the hill towards us and he was able to swing wide and miss the mattress. I gained a few more gray hairs in that incident. My young driver deserved a pat on the back and a passing grade. These unexpected occurrences are great lessons for new drivers.

They are reminders that on the road, you should expect anything. At least it wasn't a king-size mattress!

There was a day when I received a call from a former Yugoslavian who now lived in Hot Springs. He told me that if I came to Hot Springs and taught his wife to drive, he would give me a bottle of Champagne. If she managed to obtain her license, he would reward me with a gold chain.

Hot Springs is about an hour's drive from Little Rock and this was not too far for me to drive. So, every time I drove to Hot Springs and gave her a lesson, he gave me a bottle of Champagne. I must have driven over there five or six times. The last time, we decided that she was ready to take the test. Unfortunately, the test made her so nervous that she did not pass it. After I took her home, the husband kicked me out. He said she would never get to drive. I felt so bad for her. If given another lesson, she would have passed. And passing the test would have given her a way to leave her abusive husband. Despite that champagne, this story did not have a happy ending.

*When learning to drive it is important for students to experience a variety of situations while with a driving instructor. I exposed them to as many situations as possible before they experienced them on their own. This helped build student confidence, situational awareness and decision-making skills.*

Another resident of Hot Springs called to ask whether I would go there to teach him to drive. He had only one good eye, and a patch covered his bad eye. He was in his late forties and had never learned to drive. When I arrived at his home, I found he was living with his mother and he invited me in to meet her. It was a weird sensation for me to see that their furniture was covered with sheets. This was really strange and kind of scary, as you might imagine. I thought, what have I gotten myself into?

I never found out why the furniture was covered, but I enjoyed my time with this unusual student. He actually caught on to the knack of driving in just a few lessons. I didn't learn how he lost an eye, and I returned to Hot Springs only three times. This reinforced the adage to never to judge a book by its cover. The experience helped me realize that I was teaching life-long skills to my students, while they have taught me so many things about people and life.

I once had a student in her thirties who walked everywhere she went. She had a young son, about six years old, and he often walked with her. She wanted to learn to drive so she would not have to walk everywhere. She had a personality that intrigued me. I discovered after helping her learn to drive that she was an artist and taught people to paint. She worked at Michaels, an art store, that was on Markham Street.

She applied herself to learn to drive, and eventually she was able to afford to buy a car. I can still see her at Michaels whenever I visit that store. I learned that my student had overcome a lot of challenges. Not only was she a single mom without a car, she beat cancer in her later years. You have to admire people like her. We often take people at face value without knowing all the challenges they face, and overcome.

One-on-one in the car, you can come to know students well, kids as well as adults. It is surprising what they will share. You become a therapist as well as a driving instructor. One of my students was a 14-year-old visiting his grandparents for the summer. He told me that he had been very busy that summer. He said that he was really excited about taking our driving course. He was taking an art class as well. He then told me that he was trying to decide how to tell his grandparents that he was "coming out of the closet."

As we became friends, he asked me if I thought he should tell his grandparents. I advised him that it was his decision, but I did not think it was that important for him to talk to them about it. He seemed to be quite relieved by my advice.

Kids will tell all if they trust you. I do not know if he told his grandparents, but I think I helped him get a lot off his mind, and to become a better driver.

Just before Christmas one year, I received several calls from a young woman who wanted to take driving lessons. She lived with her grandmother and said they could not afford to pay for the lessons. After she called several times and begged me, I returned her call and said "I will give you lessons for free. Merry Christmas." She was very grateful. She had some driving experience, so it took only a few lessons.

About ten years later, she came to the office looking for me. I was not there because I had retired. When she tracked me down, she told me I had made such a difference in her life and she wanted me to know it. We planned to get together for lunch one day, but she had to return to college. That was the last time I talked to her. Yet I was very gratified to know I had made a difference in her life, and I was touched that she took the time to let me know, even several years later.

The lesson in that and so many experiences in life is that, even if we are instructors, we can learn as much through listening as we do by talking. And, we never know when seemingly little things we do or say will be something people carry throughout their lives.

It was while driving along Pleasant Valley Drive in Little Rock one day to pick up a student that I got the surprise of my life. I was preparing to drive under the freeway, when a small sports car fell onto the road right in front of me from above. The car landed upside down. I stopped as fast as I could and called for help. The driver was a very big man and the firemen struggled to get him out of the car. Several weeks later, I received a call from him thanking me for calling for help. He said his car was steering strangely, and he thought that was the cause of the accident. He broke several bones, and had to have many surgeries.

*This is the location Little Rock where a vehicle dropped over the edge of a bridge right in front of me while I was driving to pick up a student for a driving lesson. I learned later that the driver had fallen asleep at the wheel.*

Years later, I was talking with an insurance agent who was familiar with this wreck. She informed me that the driver had fallen asleep at the wheel because he suffered from sleep apnea. It was not the fault of the steering wheel!

In 40 years as a driving instructor, I have been involved in only one accident, which was not my fault. The accident happened on a Sunday morning around 7:00 a.m. and we were in downtown Little Rock on Broadway, a major thoroughfare. We had the green light while passing through the intersection. Out of the corner of my eye I could see a car running the red light. Without enough time to warn my student driver, the car hit us broadsided. If she had seen him coming, my student could have stepped on the gas and driven to safety, but she didn't see him.

We were not injured and remarkably my student was not upset over the mishap. I was thankful for that. It was a good lesson for her to pay special attention when driving through a busy intersection.

I was driving with a young woman on University Avenue, when suddenly I saw smoke rising from the hood of the car. I quickly instructed the student to pull over and we jumped out, cleared away from the car and ran for assistance. By the time the fire trucks arrived, the fire had done so much damage that the car had to be towed. The car had been in the shop recently and some of the wires were crossed. That started the fire. The experience was terrifying, and it was a great lesson in thinking fast for my young student.

On one occasion, I was downtown driving with an older woman when a rain storm came up from nowhere. It was a real downpour and in a matter of minutes the water flooded into the car. My frightened student was in the driver's seat. We changed places while in the car so that I could take over. Thankfully, we were stopped in traffic, so it was not too difficult or dangerous for us to change seats. The street corner had bad drainage so the water did not run off very fast. This was another scary moment that might have ended in tragedy but ended well. We kept our heads and we were lucky.

Thompson Driving School gave lessons during the summer in the parking lots of four different private schools. These schools had large parking lots so we could do a lot of maneuvers. We would put four kids in the car and would switch drivers, with three in the back seat. This would be scary for the kids in the back seat because they had no idea how well, or poorly, their friends could drive. This way, they had the experience of driving, but also learned while they were observing.

One maneuver was to put goggles on the drivers and let them see whether they could miss the cones we had set up. We called these items "drunk goggles." They gave the drivers an idea of what it would look like if they were drunk while driving. This was a fun exercise and the kids loved doing it. They hit almost every cone we set up. The objective, of course, was to encourage them to never drink and drive. It was a great way to show the kids the dangers of drunk driving.

We did a lot of private teaching from the driving manual to help students pass the written test at the State Police Headquarters. We offered a classroom for this purpose, but sometimes we just took students to a McDonald's and taught them. These were usually older adults who had not taken a test in a while.

We would also let students take the test in our cars. Sometimes they didn't own a car to take the test in. Or in some cases, they did not own a car that would pass inspection at the State Police Headquarters. We either taught them first or checked them out before allowing them to use our cars.

Some of the kids who come to us for lessons have already learned to drive after their parents taught them, but they still have to learn the rules of the road. This instruction is available to them from our classroom lectures. In many cases, the lectures make them eligible for a discount on their automobile insurance if they take and pass this part of the course.

At Thompson Driving School, we worked with witness protection people. We taught them the State Police Manual which enabled them to pass the State Police written test. After they received their permit, we taught them how to drive. They were very interesting clients. I remember one woman whom a U.S. Marshal placed here without family or friends. They had arranged to fly her chow dog to Little Rock to be with her. She was so excited to see someone from home, even though it was a dog. We always had them take the test in one of our cars and they were always frightened. I guess once they got their license, the U.S. Marshal would buy them their own car.

One of my young students did not have the money to pay for his lessons. He told me that he was good at mowing grass so I devised a plan to have him mow my lawn a certain number of times for so many driving lessons. The arrangement worked out well for both of us. He learned to drive and my grass was nicely cut. Who could object to a win-win situation?

One of the first lessons I gave when I started our driving school was with an older woman who lived in the Pulaski Heights neighborhood. I was taking her through Cammack Village, a tiny city within our city of Little Rock. As we were turning a corner, she stepped on the gas instead of slowing down and did not straighten the wheel. We jumped the curb and headed for a tree in the front yard of a house. I got on the brake just in time before slamming into the tree. I still remember that tree when I pass that house. It is still standing fifty years later. I learned a good lesson from the start to hit that brake fast when your student doesn't straighten the wheel. You must always be ready.

Kids are usually very respectful one-on-one in the car and they don't cause trouble at all. But here was an unusual exception. I took a young man out for the first time and he did really well behind the wheel. He was a natural. He was an adoptive son of a doctor in town. But our second lesson was a little different. We took off and he tried to turn a corner going really fast without slowing down. There must have been something wrong, I decided.

We drove a few more blocks and I decided this was not working. We changed seats and I drove him straight home. After turning him over to his dad, we discussed the problem and we discovered he was on a recreational drug, not a medical one. Needless to say, we did not do anymore lessons with that young man.

When I first started Thompson's Driving School, it was not uncommon for the older population of women in Little Rock to not drive. Their husbands did all the driving.

That became a problem for these women when their husbands passed away. They were left with no transportation. I noticed that the most important destinations for these widows were the grocery store, the beauty salon, church and doctors' offices.

At the driving school, we created a route they could follow and avoid heavy traffic. This plan was well-suited for essential destinations and they drove only to those places. We tailored their driving lessons and empowered these widows. They achieved a new level of confidence and independence they never had before.

When you spend your day in a car, you never know what to expect from the weather. One day I was at Murray Lock and Dam doing figure eights in the parking lot, teaching a student a technique called "hand over hand." All of a sudden, the employees of the dam were frantically motioning for me to stop the lesson. A tornado was headed straight in our direction.

Those thoughtful employees got us out of the car and safely in an enclosed area of the dam until the storm passed. The lesson ended, and I was thankful for the nice people at Murray Lock and Dam!

At one time, there were several exchange students who came to Little Rock to attend school and we taught many of them. During one driving session, I told a young man from Germany to crack the window. Of course, I meant for him to roll the window down.

He looked at me with a puzzled expression and asked, "Do you really want me to break the window?" I quickly learned one has to be careful using words when speaking with someone whose native language is not English.

These students had permission to only drive with us, so after they finished their lessons they took the driving test in our cars. They were a joy to teach for they were especially happy for the chance to learn to drive. In their own countries, students had to wait until they were much older to get a license. They were sixteen when they learned to drive at Thompson Driving School.

We also taught a group of nurses from London who worked at Arkansas Children's Hospital. Little Rock had a shortage of nurses at the time, so they were recruited to spend six months. Coincidentally, my high school coach's wife was in charge of bringing the nurses to Little Rock. We had to teach them to drive on the opposite of the road. That was a difficult habit for them to break.

I taught a woman from China the correct way to turn the steering wheel, which is hand-over-hand. We were practicing figure eights in a parking lot to help her learn the skill. I was so determined for her to catch on that I didn't stop for two hours. She finally asked if we could take a break. She had become so dizzy she became car sick. This taught me a good lesson: you don't stick with the same routine over and over. You have to vary the lesson if a student is not getting something, and then you come back to it later. After the student recovered, we continued the lesson and she finally caught on.

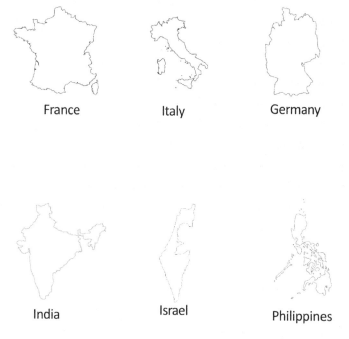

France

Italy

Germany

India

Israel

Philippines

*Through the years, Thompson Driving School has trained students from countries located around the world. Represented on this and the following page are countries some of our students called home.*

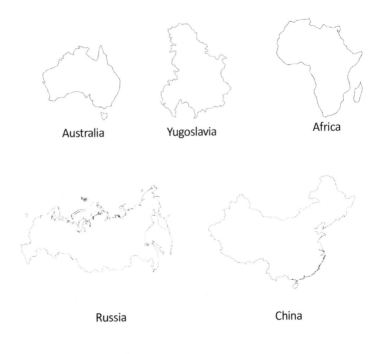

Australia

Yugoslavia

Africa

Russia

China

One of my students was from Russia and whom I really liked. A man I knew had gone to Russia to find a wife. When he returned with his wife, he immediately bought her a red convertible. There were two problems: she did not speak English, and she did not know how to drive! Yet, she was very intelligent and learned English quickly. She told me she picked up many words from watching television. She would point to the tire on the car and say "tire." Somehow, we got through the lessons without an interpreter and she learned to drive. She was a joy to work with and we became friends.

Most of our teaching took place after school and on weekends. However, home-schooled children were a big part of our business when we started. We taught these students during the day when public school students were in class. This allowed us to fill long periods during the conventional school day.

I picked up a new client at the Baptist Medical Center one day and she told me her husband was there in the hospital. I worked with her for quite a while before I found out that she had been a patient in the psychiatric unit. She was concerned I would not accept her as a student if she told me about her background. I gave her several lessons and she learned well.

To this day, I think she just wanted someone to talk to; a sympathetic listener. I've often wondered what became of her. An aspect of the business is you get attached to your students and their lives and challenges, but don't often know how their lives turn out.

I once taught a friend I first met in elementary school. She was different to me from the girl I had known. She had been a beautiful young woman during our school days, but the years had sadly taken a toll on her. She evidently had a very hard life. She asked me to drive with her to the cemetery where her parents were buried. We drove through the cemetery until we came to her parents' grave where we stopped and got out of the car. She began to explain to them that I was teaching her to drive.

After talking with her for two hours over the remainder of her lesson, I decided that she had some mental issues and probably did not need to be behind the wheel. It is always good seeing an old friend but it can also be sad.

One year, our school taught kids participating in a program called Youth Challenge. Youth Challenge is an organization sponsored by the Arkansas National Guard. They work with 16-to-18-year-olds who have been expelled from public school due to behavioral issues. They are given a chance to graduate if they learn to follow the rules.

These were troubled kids and learning to drive was very important to them, so they responded to our lessons very well and as a result had a good experience. I like to think that we contributed positively to their lives and helped them overcome some of the issues and challenges they faced.

Little Rock is home to the Arkansas Diocese of the Catholic Church. From time to time they would bring priests from Italy, France, Africa and other places to Little Rock for an extended time to serve at our Catholic Churches. Most did not know how to drive. The churches would call on us to work with them and teach them driving skills so they could get around in Little Rock. Sometimes we would have a language problem. In those cases we required an interpreter. Teaching driving with an interpreter in the back seat was very difficult and often scary, because you did not know what the interpreter was saying. All we could do was hope the interpreter got our instructions across correctly.

*This beautiful building, built in 1916, is the home of the Arkansas Diocese of the Catholic Church. Many people in the Little Rock area are not aware that it exists. From time to time while teaching corners in the Heights neighborhood, my students would see this building and ask about it. I then would have them drive through the campus and give them a little history on it.*

The driving school also had deaf students and students with vision problems. Those with eye problems had to wear special corrective lenses to be able to see while driving. The deaf students, like the foreign language students, had to have someone in the back seat who could sign. This arrangement made it extremely challenging for the instructor. The instructor also had to learn some sign language before proceeding with the lesson to ensure safety. The most important signs were "stop" and "go."

While there are all kinds of people in the world, they all have an interest in and need to be able to drive. It was up to us to be flexible and provide them that opportunity.

We had more male instructors than female and at times overly protective mothers were nervous about their daughters getting into a car alone with a man. Any parent can understand and empathize with this concern. I know I sure can.

To alleviate parents' concerns, I made a habit of providing them extensive background information on each instructor. One mother even brought her camera and took a picture of my instructor. Another mother followed our driver in her car through the whole lesson. That is, until she got lost!

Students never want to drive in the rain for their lessons. In the event of rain, it was not unusual for parents to call and try to cancel. We always told them they were lucky to get a lesson in the rain. Of course, rain is a fact of life and students are better off learning about it in a controlled environment than facing it alone for the first time.

Driving in the rain is much more dangerous than driving in clear, dry conditions. Drivers cannot see as well in the rain for one thing. The roads are very slick with the oils that have spilled onto them from passing vehicles is another hazard many new drivers are not aware of. The oils mix with the rain and makes for a dangerous surface on which hydroplaning is a real hazard.

We could usually talk students into going for their lesson in this challenging weather and they were thankful for the opportunity, for that's what it was.

I still chuckle when I think about the time one of our instructors called the office for help. She discovered her student had head lice! She was understandably panicked and didn't know what to do. We told her to return the student to her home and then come straight to the office. We then went to the store together and bought everything we needed to disinfect the car. Our unfortunate instructor had to change clothes when she returned and we provided a change of clothes for her. We sprayed the car down and left it closed and isolated for a few days.

That was something that had never happened to us before and in so far as I know, has not happened again. It goes to show there is always a first time for everything.

One of our adult students got so nervous at the wheel that the sweat was pouring from his hands. He gripped the wheel so tight that it made him sweat. This lasted for at least half of his lesson before he settled down and dried up.

I also had a young woman who hyperventilated for part of her lesson. She would just not settle down. Learning to drive is a very scary experience for some people. Building confidence is the key to getting learners to relax and learn to drive properly.

While these were extreme cases, it was not in the least bit unusual for students to have fear that affected their ability to learn to drive.

Sometimes the most difficult part of teaching people to drive is overcoming extreme anxiety and apprehension. We always wanted our students to be alert and aware, but that does not mean they need to be fearful. It was my experience that if we could address fear first that the rest of the instructional process was easier. Even more importantly, it was safer.

There was a time when I was teaching a 15-year-old girl to drive and we were in an established, quiet residential neighborhood in Little Rock.

The lesson was proceeding normally when she slammed on the brake. It turned out she was trying to avoid a squirrel that darted out in front of us. Needless to say, we paused the lesson to have a talk then about never slamming on your brake for an animal. While I love animals as much as the next person, avoiding them and risking one's own life as well as the lives of others is dangerous.

We had a student who had once been in a coma for two months from a bike accident. We worked with him for six hours before his mother decided to tell us that he was blind in one eye.

It can be amazing what parents fail to tell us that we should know before training their child. This could have resulted in a tragic outcome and I was so relieved it didn't. Over time, I learned to ask some critical questions on the front end of the process so as to avoid issues before they came up and presented a dangerous situation.

As I mentioned earlier, after they were adults each of my four children at one time or another taught driving to our students. Such was the case with one of my daughters who was an instructor for a short period.

It was during this period that one young man fell in love with my daughter and decided that taking driver training from her would be one way to be in her company. Yes, he would call just to take a lesson from her. The fact she was twice his age did not seem to matter to him. Besides, he was a very attentive student who learned the right way to drive!

Another of my favorite students was named Julie. She was about thirty years old and she had never driven. She worked downtown, so she rode the bus to work every day and to her other destinations. We worked several hours with Julie. I loved the statement she made to me on her last lesson. She said, "When I get my license, I want to have a party and I will invite all of the bus drivers of Little Rock."

Then there was the young woman who was relocating to California to get married and she needed to pass her driving test to get her license before she left. She did not own a car and wondered whether she could rent one of our cars to take her driving test.

After confirming she could drive, we allowed her to take the test in our car. I will never forget the excitement when she passed her test. She got out of the car, and she threw me a bill of $100 for payment and then ran to meet her future husband. That was a lot of money at the time for the use of our car.

When we first started Thompson Driving School, an elderly student took an entire year to learn to drive. She finally got it, with our patience and her determination, but it was a struggle for all of us. We never gave up on her, and she never gave up on herself.

I worked for several years with an orthopedic doctor's family. They had five children and his wife always said that I could not retire until I had taught all of her children. I actually got to teach the last child before I retired.

This family was among what we call "multi-generational" clients. I am proud to say that there are many families for whom we have taught students who became parents who sent their children for driver training, and ultimately those parents sent their children to us. That continues to be the case for Thompson Driving School. It seems appropriate that a multi-generational family business would serve multi-generational client families.

I once taught a seventy-eight-year-old man from Batesville, Arkansas who had never driven. Older students like him are so rewarding and so much fun to work with. They are very appreciative of the help you give them that enables them to drive a car for the first time in their lives.

Among my students was a middle-aged cardiologist from Baltimore where they have such good public transportation that he never had to learn to drive. However, when he moved to Little Rock to further his studies, he quickly learned that he needed driving lessons. He later returned to Baltimore where he probably did not use his driving skills as much, but at least he knew how to drive.

When you are driving all over town as an instructor, you see all sorts of things that you might otherwise miss. One time we saw a man beating up a woman. We called the police to help her.

Another time we spotted a man running around downtown in his underwear. On yet another occasion, we encountered a heavily intoxicated man and called the police to help him.

Crazy stuff can happen in the city, often outside the eyes and experience of our students. In taking students throughout the city, we often exposed them to places, people and situations they would otherwise miss.

For example, there is a church in the downtown section of Little Rock that has a food ministry. It is not uncommon to see people lined up to receive the basic necessity of one meal. For many young people, they are seeing a side of life they never knew existed. Thus, they not only receive instruction in driving, they receive life lessons that can broaden their horizons and perhaps prompt them to serve those in less fortunate circumstances.

**I** taught a young woman from the Philippines a long time ago. Her future husband had brought her to the United States to be his bride.

Fast forward a few years to when I ran into her at a local department store where she was a salesperson. She recognized me right away and was as pleased to see me as I was surprised to see her.

I was gratified to learn that since her driving instruction years before, she had raised a daughter who was of an age to enroll in driver training from Thompson Driving School.

# Conclusion

After a young person takes lessons from us, we always hear that they often correct their parents' driving habits. The student is now convinced that they know more than their parents.

A real joy for us as instructors is to see a student who has never driven advance from being a scared young person to become very confident behind the wheel.

I still live in Little Rock and when I pass certain houses, I think about the children who lived there. At 14, they get in our car scared to death, yet also very excited. They did not know me and had no idea what to expect from their lessons. Then I got to know them and win their trust.

Now that I have retired and my students have grown to adulthood, it gives me pause that when I go to the doctor or dentist or other venues, I see "my" 14-yr-olds all grown up and thriving in their lives and careers.

My optometrist is one of those students. So is a television personality I watch on the news. Another student went on to become a presidential press secretary.

There are many other students who have gone on to establish themselves in life and careers in their own right. But I am most proud of having taught six of my nine grandchildren to drive. They are the students I love, admire and cherish the most.

After teaching over the years, I look back and think of the many things that have meant so much to me. Learning to drive is life-changing for children as well as adults. When you are teaching 14-year-olds, it is a beginning of their independence. For adults, it might mean a way to get a job or get to work. Some of these lessons can be a real challenge, but that makes it even more worthwhile in the end. This is something that they will do for the rest of their lives. I will always be thankful for all the memories and friendships that I made.

It is the kinds of experiences I've shared that made my life and career behind the wheel such a rich and rewarding experience.

I wouldn't trade it for anything.

Made in the USA
Coppell, TX
15 July 2021

58998100R00056